A Platypus, Probably

Sneed B. Collard III

Illustrated by Andrew Plant

❦ Charlesbridge

For Mark and Jennifer,
my favorite "river rats."
—Sneed

For Mei-Yen, Su-Yen, and Piper,
I hope there will always be platypuses for
them to see.
—A. P.

Published by Charlesbridge
85 Main Street
Watertown, MA 02472
(617) 926-0329
www.charlesbridge.com

Library of Congress Cataloging-in-Publication Data
Collard, Sneed B.
    A platypus, probably / Sneed B. Collard III ; illustrated by Andrew
Plant.
        p. cm.
    ISBN 1-57091-583-0 (reinforced for library use)
    ISBN 1-57091-584-9 (softcover)
1. Platypus—Juvenile literature. I. Plant, Andrew, ill. II. Title.
QL737.M72C65 2005
599.2'9—dc22   2004018957

Printed in China
(hc) 10 9 8 7 6 5 4 3 2 1
(sc) 10 9 8 7 6 5 4 3 2 1

Illustrations done in acrylic gouache on acid-free cartridge paper
Display type and text type set in Elroy and Weiss
Color separated, printed, and bound by Jade Productions
Production supervision by Brian G. Walker
Designed by Susan Mallory Sherman

What is that strange creature,
Paddling down an Australian stream?
With its legs straight out,
And its eyes and ears closed tight,
Half lizard, half beaver,
What could it be?

A platypus, probably.

One hundred ten million years ago,
In ancient Gondwanaland,
Platypus ancestors swam through steamy forests
And tickled the feet of dinosaurs.

Gondwanaland, or Gondwana, was an ancient
supercontinent consisting of present-day Africa,
South America, Antarctica, Australia, and India.
By about 65 million years ago, these land masses
had drifted apart to become the continents and
places we know today.

Today the dinosaurs are gone.
But the platypus remains,
A warm-blooded mammal,
Different from all others.

Even though platypuses are warm-blooded, their
body temperatures are about nine degrees cooler
than most mammals. These lower temperatures
help keep platypuses from getting chilled in the
cool streams where they hunt.

That incredible bill!
Shaped like a duck's, but soft like leather,
It is packed with hundreds of tiny cells
That feel touch and even electric currents
From the bodies of other animals.

Waving its bill back and forth,
And using its wonderful webbed feet to swim,
The platypus explores eucalyptus-lined streams.
When its bill touches another animal,
Or feels the electricity from its body,
The platypus attacks.

When a platypus dives underwater, it keeps
its eyes and ears closed. Instead, it relies on
its bill and sense of touch. While hunting, the
platypus waves its bill back and forth.
Scientists believe this motion may increase
the chances of the platypus encountering
prey or detecting other animals' electric
currents. Platypuses often pause to stir up
prey by digging through gravel and mud on
stream or lake bottoms.

Worms, mussels, shrimps, tadpoles,
Even the larvae of insects found walking around the river bottom—
The platypus stuffs them all in its cheek pouches
And carries them to the surface.

An adult platypus weighs about five pounds.
It eats a huge amount of food—up to 30 percent
of its body weight each day. It stores much of its
food reserves as fat in its chubby tail.

With no teeth for chewing,
The platypus crushes its food
On hard grinding pads inside its bill.
Meal finished, it swallows,
Takes a breath,
And dives again.

Platypuses breathe air just like we do. While
hunting, platypuses usually remain underwater for
20 to 40 seconds at a time. Then they surface to
refill their lungs.

Ten, twelve hours a night, the platypus dives and paddles.
Always searching. Always hungry.
Two tight layers of fur keep it warm
In the chilly streams.

Platypus fur is even denser than the fur of polar bears and river otters. A platypus spends a lot of time cleaning and combing this fur so that it will stay waterproof and keep the platypus warm. Most people think Australia is always warm, but southern Australia can get quite cold, especially in winter. Even in tropical areas, Australian streams can be downright chilly, especially for an animal spending hours and hours underwater.

But even the platypus must stop to rest, now and then.
One moment we see its brown, swimming shape.
The next, it disappears
Into one of many hidden burrows it has dug with curving claws.

Burrows help keep a platypus safe from predators
while it is resting. The platypus's predators include
foxes, cats, monitor lizards, birds of prey, dogs,
and carpet pythons.

While the sun tracks across the Australian sky
And kangaroos forage along the banks,
The platypus sleeps.

One platypus can have up to a dozen resting burrows
along its stretch of river. Burrow entrances are dug
into the stream bank or riverbank and are almost
always hidden under overhangs, behind bushes, or
even underwater. Resting burrows can be between
three and 30 feet long.

When dusk arrives, it wakes
And slips back into the stream,
Covering miles,
Alone,
Under the patient moon,
Till dawn.

Platypuses paddle mostly with their front legs.
They use their hind legs and tails to steer. Both
their front and hind feet are webbed like a duck's.

But for platypuses,
Spring brings a new routine.
Two males see a female
And squabble over the chance to mate with her.
Armed with a venomous spur on each hind leg,
The males fight. Only one of them wins.

In sparkling waters,
The male and female circle around each other
In a courtship dance.

After several days, they mate.
Then the male swims away.

Soon the female platypus digs a nesting burrow
Up to 60 feet long.
At its end lies a nesting chamber
That she packs with leaves
Carried under her grasping tail.
Everything ready, she crawls into her retreat
And seals herself safely inside.

The female platypus doesn't give birth
Or raise babies in a pouch.
Unlike almost every other living mammal,
She lays eggs—
One, two, sometimes three precious jewels.

Mammals that lay eggs are called monotremes.
Monotremes lived on Earth at least 100 million years ago.
Today only the platypus and two species of echidnas
remain. The platypus lives only in Australia. Echidnas live
in Australia and Papua New Guinea.

For a dozen days
The female platypus curls around her eggs,
Incubating them.
Keeping them safe.

Finally, the "platipups" hatch
And slurp milk from their mother's belly.

Platypuses don't have nipples like other mammals. Instead, milk oozes out of two patches of skin on the mother's stomach and drips down strands of fur to the babies' hungry mouths.

The platypus babies grow fast.
At six weeks of age,
All covered with fur,
They open their eyes,
Ready to poke their heads
Into the world.

Platypuses can live up to 17 years in captivity but usually only four to eight years in the wild.

After four or five months,
They drink the last of their mother's milk.
And on one dusky evening,
They set off into the stream
To find their own territories
Full of food and shelter.

Male and female platypuses seem to need different amounts of living space. In one study, male platypuses were found to use about three miles of stream for their activities. Females used much less—only about half a mile. Platypuses, though, can travel long distances. A young male platypus that was trapped and tagged in one location was found almost 30 miles away seven months later.

One swims past a fisherman and his son.
"What is that?" the boy asks.
The man scratches his chin.
He smiles.

The Australian government has passed laws completely
protecting platypuses from hunting, collecting, and other
harmful human activities.

"A platypus, probably."

Nature's Improbable Wonder

Scientists believe that platypuses and other monotremes may be closely related to reptiles. One hundred million years ago many kinds of monotremes lived on earth. Eventually, however, most monotremes were crowded out by mammals that gave birth to live babies. Platypuses probably survived because Australia had fewer large mammalian predators than other continents and because platypuses evolved unique features that allowed them to hunt and live in freshwater streams.

Unfortunately many of the streams that platypuses once lived in have been destroyed or damaged by human development and pollution. As a result you won't find many platypuses close to cities. However, the animals survive in many of eastern Australia's wilder streams, lakes, and rivers.

Australians are taking steps to help platypuses. These steps include improving water quality, removing obstacles that might trap or drown platypuses, replacing weedy vegetation along stream banks with native eucalyptus and acacia trees, and stabilizing stream banks to prevent erosion. These actions are paying off. Platypus numbers have recently increased in some streams, and there are plans to reintroduce platypuses into places they haven't lived in decades.

To learn more about the platypus, explore the website of the Australian Platypus Conservancy at http://www.totalretail.com/platypus.

Glossary

Gondwanaland The ancient supercontinent that consisted of present-day Africa, South America, Antarctica, Australia, and India joined together. Eventually these landmasses separated into the continents and countries we know today.

larva (plural: **larvae**) The young or early stage of some animals. Caterpillars, for instance, are the larvae of butterflies and moths.

monotremes An ancient group of mammals that lay eggs. Today only the platypus and echidna remain.

supercontinent A large continent consisting of several smaller continents or landmasses joined together.

venomous Able to inject poison into another animal.

warm-blooded Able to generate one's own body heat.